Sled Dog Wisdom

Revised Second Edition

Collected by

Tricia Brown

Epicenter Press Inc.
Alaskan Book Adventures

Sled Dog Wisdom
Humorous and Heartwarming Tales
of Alaska's Mushers

Revised Second Edition 2016

Collected by Tricia Brown

Published by
Epicenter Press

Epicenter Press is a regional press publishing nonfiction books about the arts, history, environment, and diverse cultures and lifestyles of Alaska and the Pacific Northwest.

For more information, visit www.EpicenterPress.com.

Library of Congress Control Number: 2015959096

ISBN: 978-1-935347-52-1

10 9 8 7 6 5 4 3 2 1

Printed in the United States of America

Book and cover design, Jeanie James, www.Shorebird-Creative.com

For the dogs,
who worship unworthy gods.

Introduction

The mushers themselves are very aware that it is the dogs, not the mushers, who deserve the accolades. They possess such grace and grit, silliness and devotion. We fans are awed by their abilities, the enthusiasm and sheer power in their sleek bodies.

It's also true that few of us could manage what the mushers do. It takes ambition, stamina, strategy, and financial sacrifice. But the mushers make the headlines and sound bites. They get pats on the back from their sponsors, see fans lining up for autographs, and accept the occasional fat check or, for the champions, a shiny new truck. And there's the pride of seeing their dogs achieve after hundreds of miles of training. All well-deserved.

The dogs? They get a garland of yellow roses, a cushier dog box, designer dog food, a top-of-the-line harness. But their supreme payback is getting to run, and run, and run, with the man or woman they hold in greatest esteem. Of course, the feeling is mutual. We've all seen press coverage of careworn mushers at the finish line, on their knees before their lead dogs in a speechless hug.

Mushers and dogs do share a unique relationship—well beyond "pet and master," neither son or daughter, nor BFFs. At the start line, they're more like coach and fine-tuned athletes. Sled dogs already know how to run. It's hard-wired. And their trainers are surely addicted to the sport and emotionally sold out to their top dogs. So they teach each other, trust each other, carry each other.

We asked dozens of mushers—in long-distance, middle-distance, sprint, and recreational mushing—what they've learned from owning and running sled dogs. That's what this book is about: confessions of mushers who are not surprised about who's teaching whom, and who deserves the greater praise.

Teamwork

We're a pack and I'm the alpha male. No more, no less. They do their part, I do my part, and we're a team.

— **Charlie Boulding,** Manley, Alaska
Two-time Yukon Quest champion;
Kuskokwim 300 champion, Kobuk 440 champion;
Iditarod veteran, finishing in the Top Ten eight times

It's like a coach on a ball team. You've got to put the players in the right positions, work with them, get the most out of what you've got to work with. It's a challenge to put all these individuals together and make a competitive team.

— **Joe Redington, Jr.,** Manley Hot Springs, Alaska Iditarod and sprint veteran, winning Fur Rendezvous World Championship, Yukon River Championship; top three in North American Championship; Arctic Circle Championship

---

"Thank God Charlie's got the right trail," CHRISTOPHER KNOTT thought as his lead dog finally spied a trail marker through a swirling snowstorm along the Bering Sea. For a while, the Iditarod musher had no idea where he was headed. After three hours of creeping along, Knott's leaders, Hotfoot and Charlie, suddenly stopped. "What's going on?!" Knott wondered. The snow was blowing so hard, he could barely see past the end of his sled, let alone to his leaders. He set his ice hook and struggled to the front of the team. There he discovered Charlie standing on the very steps of the checkpoint. "I have no idea why he went to that building. He'd never been there before," Knott said.

Mushing dogs is a game of feet. You really learn how important it is to take care of the dogs' feet.

— **Mark Weber,** Anchorage, Alaska
Former Dillingham competitive musher

I accept this award on behalf of all mushers still on the trail, in the middle of the night, far from the checkpoint, on their hands and knees, taking care of their dogs. Nobody's talking, nobody's sleeping, nobody's eating. Their moving up and down the line of dogs, taking care of little aches and pains.

— **Dave Olesen,** Great Slave Lake, Canada
Bush pilot and musher, accepting the Alyeska Vet's Choice Award,
1998 Yukon Quest

Have faith in your team.

— **Andy Willis,** Wasilla, Alaska
Two-time Iditarod finisher, Bush pilot, big-game hunting guide

Photo © Fotolia.com

From running dogs I've learned how the different parts of a team work together. You've got lead dogs wheel dogs, swing dogs, and team dogs, and they all have to fulfill their particular function for the team to do well. Just like in life, we all have our part.

— **Daryl Hollingsworth,** Seward, Alaska
Sprint-racing champion

If they ain't got no one for them to follow, they won't go.
— **Michael King,** Salcha, Alaska
Yukon Quest musher, operates Alaska Trail King Adventures

Photo © Bigstockphoto.com

If you are good to dogs, they are good to you. They'll do all they can to help you.

— **Job Noachuck,** Kokochuruk, Alaska
Nome elder (1917-2008);
mushed working dogs on hunting trips and wood hauls

In the old days, the dog care was different. The food was different. Feed your dogs dried fish and beaver, and they went all right.

— **Rudy Demoski,** Wasilla, Alaska
Yup'ik, 1974 Iditarod rookie;
veteran sprint and distance musher

With sled dogs came life lessons for all the Seaveys who have pursued them even now, into the fourth generation. It has all been there: breeding, birth of pups, deaths of old and loyal animals, dog chores, medical needs, race competition sportsmanship, defeat, setbacks, perseverance, and the handling of success. All of this and a good deal more. All there for the learning because there are sled dogs for the teaching.

— **Dan Seavey,** Seward, Alaska
Participant in inaugural Iditarod (and thereafter);
patriarch in a growing clan of champion mushers;
operates Seavey's Ididaride Sled Dog Tours

A good dog can teach your team more than you could ever teach your team.

— **Robb Carss,** Alberta, Canada
Iditarod rookie in 1996

Learning from Our Mistakes Together

Your dogs are always right. The dogs never make mistakes. When we try to make them do something they've never been taught, we make mistakes.

— **Howard Farley,** Nome, Alaska

Helped organize and ran the first Iditarod in 1973;co-founded the new Nome Kennel Club

As you get older, you get a little smarter.

— **Joe Redington,** Sr., Knik, Alaska (1917-1999)

Father of the Iditarod, completed the 25th Iditarod at age 80

Some dogs have to learn the hard way. Iditarod musher JOHN BARRON found this out on the year his leader, Oogruk, was headed toward a hole in the ice. Barron gave Oogruk a "Gee" to go right. "He didn't take the gee, and he slipped into the hole," Barron remembers. *The river current was so strong that the dog was being pushed under the ice and its harness was slipping off. With his heart pounding, Barron flipped his sled on its side and hurried forward. He reached in, grabbed a handful of skin and harness, and pulled Oogruk to safety.* "After that, when I said 'Gee,' when I said 'Haw,' he was right there!"

Never set your expectations too high if you're a rookie in a long-distance race. You'll be humbled quickly.

— **Brenda Mackey,** Nenana, Alaska
Third-generation distance racer,
after her 1998 Yukon Quest rookie run

I've never been involved in a sport that will take you through so many different emotions in such a short time. You can be going along on a beautiful run, on a great day, and your dogs running well, thinking 'This is a great team.' And you round a corner and things suddenly go haywire—it can happen so quickly!

— **Keli Mahoney,** Talkeetna, Alaska (1968-2003)
Iditarod and Yukon Quest musher, firefighter, and private pilot

"Keep your guard up," says sprint racer NITA HOLLINGSWORTH, even when you believe the worst part of the trail is behind you. As a teenager in the 1994 Junior World Championship, the Seward musher had safely taken several treacherous corners at high speeds. She cracked up when she least expected it – on the straightaway. "I hit a stump sticking up out of the snow. My sled shot into the air, and so did I. I woke up lying in the snow with a busted sled, busted arm, and no dogs."

My hard-earned lesson: Never turn your back on the dogs. Or they'll be long gone.

— **Don Honea,** Ruby, Alaska
Athabascan First Traditional Chief,
Iditarod veteran, who with Howard Albert and Emmitt Peters,
was one of three Ruby mushers
who placed in the 1979 Iditarod Top Ten

Having a Laugh

I've learned how to keep my balance when I'm sleeping and how to hang on tight! (I drag pretty well.)

— **Jennifer Deye Freking,** Finland, Minnesota
Spoken as a Junior Iditarod musher;
now a kennel operator with husband Blake Freking
and veteran of the Iditarod
and John Beargrease Sled Dog Marathon

Never eat orange slices with the same gloves you wear to feed the dogs their fish snacks.

— **Linda Joy,** Kenai, Alaska
Iditarod musher

"One year I was real sick and my dogs were happy," said four-time Yukon Quest musher *LARRY CARROLL of Willow, Alaska. "They kept looking back at me and saying 'Poor son-of-a-gun.' The next year, I felt good and my dogs were sick."*

From running dogs I've gotten independence and a whole new outlook on life. Also I've learned that Ding Dongs® are the best on the trail … and Twinkies® don't freeze."

— **Lindsey Hanson,** Anchorage, Alaska
Spoken as a teenaged Junior Iditarod musher

It was the worst year you could have finished second – behind the first woman to win it.

— **Dewey Halverson,** Homer, Alaska
Second to Libby Riddles in 1985 Iditarod

The view never changes unless you're the lead dog.

— **Anonymous**

Chugiak musher JIM LANIER, whose been competing in the Iditarod since 1979, says he learned that when all is said and done, dogs will be dogs: "One real 'lowlight' of my mushing experience is when I was taking my team on a training run, and the entire team, one by one, ran through a small door and into a chicken coop. Each dog came out with a squawking chicken in its mouth."

Photo © Fotolia.com

Watch your mouth. Dogs and small children might be listening.

— **Anonymous**

The Heart
of a Sled Dog

Tomorrow is a maybe. Yesterday is a memory.
Today is a treasure.

— **Jeff King,** Denali Park, Alaska
1993, 1996, 1998, and 2006 Iditarod champion;
1989 Yukon Quest champion; numerous Top Ten finishes;
operates Husky Homestead

People don't realize how athletic the dogs are. If you did an autopsy on a race dog and a wolf … the race dog's heart is two, three times bigger; its lungs are two, three times bigger. They are superior athletes.

— **Curtis Erhart,** Fairbanks, Alaska
Fourth-generation Athabascan dog musher,
who breeds dogs for mid-distance and Iditarod;
competes with a sprint team

The harder I work, the luckier I get.

— **Martin Buser,** Big Lake, Alaska
Four-time Iditarod champion'five-time Leonhard Seppala
Humanitarian Award winner;
operates Happy Trails Kennel

Photo © Tricia Brown

The dogs are happiest when they have a job to do. You treat them right and give them a fair chance and they're just amazing.

— **Libby Riddles,** Homer, Alaska
Author, speaker, first woman to win the Iditarod, 1985

Photo © Fotolia.com

You could run this race twenty-five years in a row and never figure out how the dogs do it—how they run a thousand miles in ten or twelve days just because you've asked them to.

— **Tim Mowry,** Two Rivers, Alaska
Completed the Iditarod twice and the Yukon Quest eight times,
winning the 1992 Sportsmanship Award

Any time I'm under stress, I try to get to where the dogs are mentally – they don't care where Rick Swenson is or where Doug Swingley is. They just care about being with me.

— **Vern Halter,** Trapper Creek, Alaska
Yukon Quest champion, Iditarod veteran;
operates Dream a Dream Kennel

My dogs have taught me many of life's lessons about responsibility, passion, sportsmanship and respect.

— **Danny Seavey,** Seward, Alaska
Author, third-generation Iditarod competitor

Like children, they need daily, if not constant, attention.

— **Jim Lanier,** Chugiak, Alaska
Iditarod musher

Dogs teach you what unconditional love is all about.

— **Jack Berry,** Homer, Alaska
Distance and sprint musher;
Yukon Quest 1999 Sportsmanship Award, 2000 Dawson Award

My dogs taught me to shut up and let them do their job. On one run, I talked to my leader Socks the whole time, and finally he laid down and wouldn't get up until I shut up.

— **Kimarie Hanson,** Anchorage, Alaska
Four-time competitor in the Junior Iditarod;
ran the Iditarod at age 18

[Larry] was telling me that he could win the Iditarod if I just paid attention to him.

— **Lance Mackey,** Fox, Alaska
Referring to his famous leader who was running in wheel
when he "spoke" to Mackey during the 2009 race;
Larry would lead Mackey to his third consecutive Iditarod victory.

I've learned over the years that the dogs are smarter than humans when it comes to communication. They know what you're thinking at all times.

— **George Attla,** North Pole, Alaska (1933-2015)
Athabascan sprint icon, winning ten Fur Rendezvous Open World Championships and eight North American Open Championships; placed fourth in the first Iditarod, 1973

My dogs have taught me to not interrupt them when they're busy running.

— **Cindy Gallea,** Wykoff, Minnesota
Iditarod veteran

The dogs have taught me how easy it is to communicate with them, in all ways.

— **Bob Hickel,** Anchorage, Alaska
Distance and mid-distance musher;
winner 1992 Iditarod Sportsmanship Award

Austrian-Canadian musher HANS GATT is a four-time Yukon Quest champion and record holder, four-time Wyoming Stage Stop champion, a four-time European Championship sprint race winner, and IFSS World Championship Open Class sprint winner. He's also taken first place in numerous mid-distance races including the Copper Basin and Percy DeWolfe. You don't get to that level of racing without a few enlightening moments along the way. One year, Gatt raced borrowed dogs for Open North American Sled Dog Race in Fairbanks. The musher who loaned them advised Gatt that the dogs were whip-trained. (While the whip never really touches the dogs, they respond to the cracking sound overhead.) "We were about three miles from the line and I cracked the whip," Gatt said. "And both the leaders laid down. Turns out the owner had whip-trained them to help break up dog fights. Lying down was exactly what they were supposed to do. Gatt laughed about it later, even though, he said, "It cost me a couple of places in the race."

In the Race

Every aspect of my life has been enriched by the dogs.
I've been mushing since I was four years old, so I have
years of appreciation for them.

— **Mitch Seavey,** Seward, Alaska
Two-time Iditarod champion;
operates Seavey's Iditaride Sled Dog Tours

Watching all the energy they put forth, the dogs have
taught me to be very humble. Whether it's warm, cold,
80 mph winds, they go on. They're so dedicated.

— **David Sawatzky,** Healy, Alaska
Yukon Quest and Iditarod veteran

MARY SHIELDS of Salcha, Alaska, learned about perseverance from running dogs. She and Lolly Medley were groundbreakers when they ran the Iditarod in 1974. That was the second year of the race, but the first year for women to enter—and finish. "At the starting line, someone hollered, 'You better turn around now, you'll never make it,' " Shields recalled. "That meant for sure I was going to."

The average musher has no idea how resilient dogs are.
No matter how tough you think you are as a person, the
dogs far exceed that. That is the key to winning races.

— **Dick Mackey,** Alaska
Champion musher who competed in Iditarod's
inaugural race and, in 1978,
beat Rick Swenson by one second

Photo © Fotolia.com

I learned how to sleep comfortably. I used to sleep with my arms under my head, all curled up. Then I saw how the dogs slept stretched out. I sleep so good now.

— **Nora Gruner,** Fairbanks, Alaska
Recreational musher, elementary teacher, gardener

My dogs have taught me that it is better to go slow than
not go at all! Baby steps ... baby steps.

— **Jim Gallea,** Seeley Lake, Montana
Spoken as a Junior Iditarod musher,
who went on to run the Iditarod three times

When people comment that there are three generations
of Seaveys racing sled dogs, I always say, 'The sins of the
father are perpetuated to the successive generations.' It's
pretty gratifying, really.

— **Dan Seavey,** Sr., Seward, Alaska
Helped establish and ran inaugural Iditarod in 1973;
author, patriarch of generational champion mushers

Photo © Fotolia.com

In the spring, the yard is all mud, and the dogs are muddy and pitiful-looking. They jump around and sling wet stuff across your face, and you worry about what's mixed in with the mud. Then summer comes and the yard gets dusty. To cut down on the dust you spray the yard with water, and the mud comes back. The best part is in the fall, as you wait for snow and get all the equipment ready to go. You look forward to that first run.

— **Steve Ihde,** Anchorage, Alaska
Recreational musher

Train! If I don't train them well enough, I have to run up the hills. And I've done a lot of that! I lost twenty pounds on one race.

— **Stephen Adkins,** Trapper Creek, Alaska
Six-time Iditarod finisher

Running the Iditarod completely changed my life. It made me aware I could do anything if I put my mind to it.

— **Jon Van Zyle,** Chugiak, Alaska
Official Iditarod Artist;
two-time Iditarod finisher

It's just like old-timers say: If you make one little mistake, it can lead to a bigger mistake and a bigger mistake. You always keep that in mind – don't let this thing get out of control.

— **Joe Runyan,** Cliff, New Mexico
Author and champion of 1985 Yukon Quest;
1988 Alpirod; and 1989 Iditarod

Personality

The dogs have as much pride as any human athlete. That's why Granite was a wonderful dog. He knew when he won. He though he deserved all the accolades, he expected them. He was a ham in front of the media.

— **Susan Butcher,** Fairbanks, Alaska (1954-2006)
Four-time Iditarod champion;
drove dogs to Mt. McKinley's summit with a party in 1979

Photo © Fotolia.com

I picked out Zorro because he was the first pup out of the doghouse, he was the first one to the feed dish, and the last one to walk away. And, he was a little fur ball that would just stand his ground barking. He had to be mine.

— **Lance Mackey,** Fairbanks, Alaska
Four consecutive Iditarod wins,
four consecutive Yukon Quest wins;
first and only musher to win both races back-to-back

In his day, Solo was a main leader. He wasn't the fastest, but he was always able to get up and go. He taught me that when things are tough, that's more important.

—**Linwood Fiedler,** Willow, Alaska
Four Top-Ten finishes since 1989 rookie Iditarod

Mushers like to think of themselves as more important than they are. Humans are but one factor in the training program. The dogs teach each other more than the humans do.

— **John Wood,** Matanuska-Susitna Valley, Alaska
Sprint musher

Melissa was the only dog in history that won the Iditarod, the North American, and the Anchorage Fur Rendezvous World Championship Sled Dog Race – all for Carl.

— **Jerry Austin,** St. Michael, Alaska (1947-2010)
Iditarod Hall of Fame member, describing the 1976 Iditarod team
he assembled with help from Carl Huntington's kennel

They're working dogs, but they know when it's a race day. On working days, they're way more calm. Before a race, they bark and go wild.

— **Clement Nelson,** Kotzebue, Alaska
Iñupiaq sprint musher
who used dogs to hunt, haul wood, set up camp

A lot of people base too much on their first impression of a dog. The first impression isn't necessarily going to be accurate. A little bit shy doesn't mean the dog doesn't have a strong head. A dog that shows early promise as a leader may not have his head together.

— **Peter Butteri,** Tok, Alaska
Yukon Quest veteran;
winner of 2002 Dawson Award and Kiwanis Award

Photo © Fotolia.com

They know your innermost thoughts. My old lead dog Pal knew more about me than I knew about him.

— **Roy Monk,** Lancashire, England
Iditarod and Yukon Quest musher

Dogs are amazing animals. I just love the dogs. They have taught me a lot of responsibility [and] hard work like farming. They're always there and they're always happy to see you. And they've brought a lot of amazing people together in the fans, mushers, and volunteers.

— **Raymie Redington,** Knik, Alaska
Ten-time Iditarod finisher, second generation
in a multi-generational mushing family

When we said 'Mush!' the dogs turned around and got up on the sled, wagging their tail and wanting to be petted.

— **Norman Vaughn,** Anchorage, Alaska (1905-2005)
Life-long adventurer who was 12 in 1917,
when he first harnessed a German shepherd and a collie

Trust

Sometimes they fool me.
— **Herbie Nayokpuk,** Shishmaref, Alaska (1929-2006)
Iñupiaq musher known as "The Shishmaref Cannonball;"
Iditarod Hall of Fame member, designated an Iditarod Icon

Dogs like consistent behavior throughout training and racing. If you suddenly pull something out of the hat and make a change, that would break the trust.
— **Matt Hayashida,** Willow, Alaska
Iditarod veteran who won Sportsmanship Award in 1999

Don't second-guess your leader, especially in bad weather.
— **Ramey Smith,** Willow, Alaska
Iditarod veteran with nine finishes in the Top Ten

What I love about sled dogs is they trust you to make their decisions for them. And if you make mistakes, they still love you.

— **Gerri Hanschen,** Sebeka, Minnesota
Former president Seward Mushers and Sled Handlers

RICK MACKEY's 1998 Yukon Quest leader, Cindy, was taking the team through the Fortymile country in her second Quest when she approached a closed-up cabin that had been a checkpoint a year earlier. There were no markers or broken trail. And yet the young dog remembered the place and tried to pull in. That taught Mackey this: "Trust your leaders and you'll stay out of trouble. They know where they're going … or at least where they went last year!"

When you're tired or bummed out, the dogs bring you out of it. The things we worry about, they just don't give a hoot about.

— **Ramy Brooks,** Fairbanks, Alaska
Native Alaskan, Iditarod musher, Yukon Quest champion

The dogs have taught me to sit back and enjoy the simple things in life.

— **Dalton Fiedler,** Juneau, Alaska
Mushing veteran;
Operates Alaska Heli-Mush
with his father, Iditarod veteran Linwood Fiedler

stocphoto.com

The sled dog is your friend. You train them. And they're athletes. But you've got to be friends with them. There has to be trust. If they don't trust you, they're not going to give you what you need to be a winner.

— **Shannon Erhart,** Fairbanks, Alaska
Breeds middle-distance and Iditarod dogs;
competes on sprint circuit

Photo © Fotolia.com

You can never waste time sitting still and cuddling a puppy. That time comes back to you later in affection from the dog and its willingness to run for you.

— **DeeDee Jonrowe**, Willow, Alaska
Sixteen Top-Ten Iditarod finishes, multiple awards

Trust the dogs.

— **Paul Gebhardt,** Kasilof, Alaska
Veteran with seven Top-Ten Iditarod finishes;
multiple awards in dog care and speed

Living in the Moment

The dogs have taught me to enjoy the outdoors.

— **Ken Chase,** Anvik, Alaska
Athabascan Iditarod veteran with three Top-Ten finishes;
competed in first Iditarod, 1973

Run as best as you can, but enjoy the trip.

— **Terry Adkins,** Sand Coulee, Montana
1973 Iditarod's only veterinarian;
eighteen-time Iditarod finisher

Photo ©

A lot of people make the mistake of thinking dogs are human because they relate to their emotional characteristics. Dogs can be happy, sad, excited, or bored, but they live in the moment.

— **Lynda Plettner,** Big Lake, Alaska
Twelve-time Iditarod finisher;
self-described "Grandmother that has run the most Iditarod races"

The main thing is to have a good time. If you don't have a good time, you're in trouble because you can't always succeed in your goals.

— **Jacques Philip,** Alaska and France
Distance musher in Alaska and Europe;
three-time Alpirod champion

If you want to make your dreams come true, you must stay awake.

— **Keith Kirkvold,** Fairbanks, Alaska
Yukon Quest musher

My motto with my dogs is, 'It's a great day to be alive.'
— **Bill Snodgrass,** Dubois, Wyoming
1998 rookie Iditarod race was covered by Discovery Channel;
operates Continental Divide Dog Sled Adventures

CPSIA information can be obtained
at www.ICGtesting.com
Printed in the USA
FSOW04n0854220617
35493FS